EA-6B PROWLERS

BY CARLOS ALVAREZ

BELLWETHER MEDIA · MINNEAPOLIS, MN

Are you ready to take it to the extreme?
Torque books thrust you into the action-packed
world of sports, vehicles, and adventure. These books
may include dirt, smoke, fire, and dangerous stunts.
WARNING: read at your own risk.

Library of Congress Cataloging-in-Publication Data

Alvarez, Carlos, 1968-
  EA-6B Prowlers / by Carlos Alvarez.
      p. cm. – (Torque: military machines)
  Includes bibliographical references and index.
  Summary: "Amazing photography accompanies engaging information about EA-6B Prowlers.
The combination of high-interest subject matter and light text is intended for students in grades 3
through 7"–Provided by publisher.
  ISBN 978-1-60014-292-5 (hardcover : alk. paper)
  1. EA-6 (Electronic warfare aircraft)–Juvenile literature. I. Title.
  UG1242.E43A45 2010
  623.74'6–dc22
                                              2009008485

This edition first published in 2010 by Bellwether Media, Inc.

The photographs in this book are reproduced through the courtesy of the United States Department of
Defense.

Printed in the United States of America.

CONTENTS

THE EA-6B IN ACTION

A United States bomber plane cruises through the sky. The bomber is on a dangerous **mission**. Its target is heavily defended. The enemy will shoot down the plane if they detect it on **radar**.

15803

CVWP
NAVY
VAQ-128

The bomber isn't alone on its mission. A U.S. Navy EA-6B Prowler is in the air too. It is there to keep the bomber safe. The Prowler's crew uses advanced electronics to **jam** the enemy's radar. The Prowler sends out strong radio signals. The signals stop the enemy radar from working.

The radar jamming works. The enemy radar doesn't spot the planes. The bomber cruises over its target and drops a bomb. The target is destroyed. The two planes have completed their mission.

ELECTRONIC WARFARE AIRCRAFT

The EA-6B Prowler is an electronic warfare aircraft. It protects U.S. military forces and planes. It does this by blocking enemy radio signals. The Prowler has high-tech electronic gear. This gear can send out signals to jam enemy radar and communications.

★ FAST FACT ★

The Prowler can be refueled while still in flight.

11

The Prowler entered U.S. military service in 1971. It replaced the EKA-3B Skywarrior. The U.S. military has improved the Prowler over time. Upgrades have given the Prowler better electronics. It can now also fire **missiles**. However, the Prowler is nearing the end of its service. The U.S. Navy plans to replace it with a new plane called the F/A-18G Growler.

The U.S. Navy, Air Force, and Marine Corps all use the Prowler.

WEAPONS AND FEATURES

The most important feature of the Prowler is its **electronic countermeasures**. The plane uses a system of pods called the **ALQ-99**. This system jams enemy signals. Antennas in the plane's tail detect enemy signals. The plane's crew uses a powerful computer to jam them. Two ALQ-99 pods are mounted under each wing. A fifth pod rests under the body of the plane.

The Prowler can also fire missiles. It can take out enemy defense systems. The AGM-88 high-speed anti-radiation missile (HARM) can be fired at targets on land or water. The HARM takes out communications targets. It is used mostly against equipment that helps guide enemy missiles.

EA-6B SPECIFICATIONS:

Primary Function: Electronic countermeasures

Length: 59 feet 10 inches (17.7 meters)

Height: 16 feet 8 inches (4.9 meters)

Maximum Weight: 61,500 pounds
(27,500 kilograms)

Wingspan: 53 feet (16 meters)

Speed: 575 miles (920 kilometers) per hour

Ceiling: 37,600 feet (11,500 meters)

Engines: 2 Pratt & Whitney J52-P408 engines

Range: 1,150 miles (1,840 kilometers)

EA-6B MISSIONS

The Prowler's primary mission is to keep U.S. forces safe. It does this by jamming enemy signals. Jamming enemy radar prevents missile attacks on U.S. aircraft. The enemy cannot lock weapons on to U.S. planes. It also causes confusion. It prevents the enemy from quickly responding to an attack.

19

★ FAST FACT ★

The Prowler was based on the A-6 Intruder airframe.
The Intruder was a U.S. attack fighter from 1963 to 1997.

The Prowler has a crew of four. The pilot flies the plane. Three **electronic countermeasures officers (ECMOs)** work with the pilot. One ECMO **navigates**, operates communications, and monitors defense. This ECMO sits next to the pilot in the front of the **cockpit**. The other two ECMOs sit in the rear of the cockpit. They operate the ALQ-99 system. The four crew members work together to complete their missions. They keep the U.S. military one step ahead of its enemies.

GLOSSARY

ALQ-99—the radar-jamming system carried by the EA-6B Prowler; the ALQ-99 includes five pods that emit powerful radio signals.

cockpit—the part of an airplane in which the pilot and other crewmembers sit

electronic countermeasures—a defensive device used to confuse or jam an enemy signal

electronic countermeasures officer (ECMO)—a Prowler crew member who works with the plane's advanced electronic jamming system

jam—to block a signal by using electronic countermeasures

missile—an explosive launched at targets on the ground or in the air

mission—a military task

navigate—to find one's way in unfamiliar terrain

radar—a sensor system that uses radio waves to locate objects

TO LEARN MORE

AT THE LIBRARY

David, Jack. *The United States Navy.* Minneapolis, Minn.: Bellwether, 2008.

Hansen, Ole Steen. *The EA-6B Prowler.* Mankato, Minn.: Capstone, 2006.

Sweetman, Bill. *Radar Jammers: The EA-6B Prowlers.* Mankato, Minn.: Capstone, 2002.

ON THE WEB

Learning more about military machines is as easy as 1, 2, 3.

1. Go to www.factsurfer.com.

2. Enter "military machines" into search box.

3. Click the "Surf" button and you will see a list of related Web sites.

With factsurfer.com, finding more information is just a click away.

INDEX